Classic

CHINESE

Classic
CHINESE

Authentic dishes from the orient

FOREWORD BY
DEH-TA HSIUNG

SMITHMARK

© 1996 Anness Publishing Limited

This edition published in 1996 by
SMITHMARK Publishers, a division of US Media Holdings, Inc
16 East 32nd Street
New York NY 10016
USA

SMITHMARK books are available for bulk purchase for sales promotion and for premium use. For details write or call
the Manager of Special Sales, SMITHMARK Publishers, 16 East 32nd Street, New York, NY 10016; (212) 532–6600.

Produced by Anness Publishing Limited
1 Boundary Row
London SE1 8HP

ISBN 0-8317-7378-2

Publisher Joanna Lorenz
Senior Cookery Editor Linda Fraser
Cookery Editor Anne Hildyard
Designer Nigel Partridge
Illustrations Madeleine David
Photographers Karl Adamson, Edward Allwright, Steve Baxter, James Duncan,
Michelle Garrett, Amanda Heywood and Michael Michaels
Recipes Alex Barker, Roz Denny, Rati Fernandez, Christine France,
Shirley Gill, Deh-Ta Hsiung, Liz Trigg and Steven Wheeler
Food for photography Elizabeth Wolf-Cohen, Carole Handslip, Wendy Lee and Jane Stevenson
Stylists Madelaine Brehaut, Michelle Garrett, Maria Kelly, Blake Minton and Kirsty Rawlings
Jacket photography Amanda Heywood

Typeset by MC Typeset Ltd, Rochester, Kent
Printed and bound in China

Pictures on frontispiece, 7, 8 and 9: Zefa Pictures Ltd.

CONTENTS

FOREWORD

hinese cooking is the most popular ethnic food, not just in the West, but also in every other part of the world. Chinese food, with its unique flavors and cooking techniques, has an inherent appeal. It is also both economical and healthy: because most ingredients are cut into small pieces before being cooked very quickly, they retain their natural flavors and nutrients.

Despite all the foreign influences and technological advances which have affected nearly all walks of life in China, the indigenous cuisine remains remarkably resistant to drastic change. Although foreign foodstuffs have been introduced into China for many centuries, they have become integral ingredients in many Chinese dishes.

A Chinese cook abroad can always produce a Chinese meal, even when using only local produce, for the essential "Chineseness" of the food depends entirely on *how* it is prepared and cooked, not *what* ingredients are used.

The most distinctive feature in Chinese cooking is the emphasis on the harmonious blending of color, aroma, flavor, and texture, both in a single dish and in all the dishes that make up a meal. Food preparation is another important element: it is essential that ingredients be cut into uniform shapes and sizes, whether these be small thin slices, shreds, or cubes. This is done not only for the sake of the appearance of the finished dish, but also because ingredients of a similar size and shape require about the same amount of cooking time.

Forty easy-to-follow recipes from many different regions of China have been selected for this book. I have contributed to the collection myself, and would like to commend all the dishes for you to try at home.

Bon appetit! Or, as we say in China, *Ching, Ching!*

DEH-TA HSIUNG

INTRODUCTION

China is a vast country. Stretching from the sub-arctic north to the tropical south, the different climatic zones and landscapes have given rise to a number of distinct cuisines, some of which are only now becoming known in the West. While we have become familiar with Cantonese cooking, with its sweet-and-sour treatment of pork and shrimp, and its use of fresh vegetables and fruit, our experience of the cuisine of northern Beijing tends to be limited to Peking duck and Crispy Aromatic Duck (see the recipe on page 32). The coastal

provinces around Shanghai are known for fish dishes, and wheat, rice, soybeans, and vegetables are also grown here. In the south-west, in Szechuan, hot and spicy dishes characterize the regional style of cooking.

Cooking methods also vary from province to province. Meat is either cooked slowly by braising or steaming or quickly stir-fried, whereas poultry dishes are either crispy (having been deep-fried) or tender and moist (having been simmered). Whole fish such as garoupa are often steamed with aromatics such as ginger and scallions, while seafood, especially shrimp and scallops, are stir-fried briefly so that they retain maximum moisture and flavor. Vegetables play a vital role, and the use of fresh produce is very important in Chinese cooking.

Specialist ingredients include glutinous rice, and a wide range of noodles, including egg, rice and cellophane noodles. Protein-rich soybeans are used extensively, in pastes, purées, sauces, and the increasingly popular tofu. Soy sauce is now available in various strengths, from the delicately flavored light soy sauce to the more salty dark variety. Dark soy sauce gives a rich color to a dish; where it is desirable not to mask natural colors, the lighter sauce is used. Yellow bean sauce and black bean sauce are also

Dried fish of every variety are on sale at this open-air stall in a street in Macau (far left) while persimmons and pomegranates are some of the exotic fruits on offer at a roadside market (left). On the Li river (above), fishermen set off into a lovely sunset.

made from soybeans, but are thicker than soy sauce. Black bean sauce is a special favorite and is often cooked with pork, fish, or seafood. Preserved black beans are very salty – they are usually mashed into the sauce at the end of cooking. The range of sauces includes hoisin, which has a hot, sweet flavor (excellent as a marinade for spare ribs) and oyster sauce. There is also a red bean paste, which is used as a dip or spread on the pancakes served with Peking duck, and chili paste, which is made from chilies, soybeans, salt, sugar, and flour.

Tofu – pressed soybean curd – is available in various forms, from soft to firm, and can be cubed or sliced. Smoked firm tofu is also on sale. Specialist oils, like the nutty sesame oil and the fiery chili oil, can also be used to add flavor to a dish, but, as the foreword to this book suggests, harmony is very important in the composition of both single dishes and entire Chinese meals. No sauce should dominate, and colors, flavors, aromas, and textures should be in balance.

Chinese food is easy to prepare at home, especially now that the ingredients needed are so readily available. Even the smallest supermarket carries an extensive range, so familiarize yourself with this book, get out your wok and steamer, and you will soon be enjoying the diverse tastes and authentic flavors offered by *Classic Chinese*.

MARBLED QUAIL'S EGGS

ard-boiled quail's eggs reboiled in smoky China tea assume a pretty marbled skin. Dip them into a fragrant spicy salt and hand them round with drinks, or serve them as a starter. Szechuan peppercorns can be bought from oriental food shops.

INGREDIENTS
12 quail's eggs
2½ cups strong lapsang souchong tea
1 tablespoon dark soy sauce
1 tablespoon dry sherry
2 whole star anise
frisée, milled Szechuan peppercorns, and sea salt, to serve

SERVES 4–6

1 Place the quail's eggs in a saucepan of cold water and bring to a boil. Time them for 2 minutes from the moment when the water comes to a boil.

2 Transfer the eggs from the pan to a colander and run them under cold water to cool. Tap the shells all over so they are crazed, but do not peel the eggs.

COOK'S TIP
Szechuan peppercorns are dried reddish brown berries from a shrub native to Szechuan. They are not so hot as the true peppercorn, but have a numbing effect and a distinctive aroma. They are roasted, milled, and the husks discarded before use.

3 In a large saucepan, bring the tea to a boil, then add the soy sauce, sherry, and star anise. Add the eggs and boil again for about 15 minutes, partially covered, so the liquid does not boil dry.

4 Remove the eggs from the pan. When they are cool, peel and arrange on a small platter lined with frisée.

5 Mix the milled Szechuan peppercorns with an equal quantity of salt and place the mixture in a small dish to serve with the peeled eggs.

GARLIC MUSHROOMS

T ofu is high in protein and very low in fat, so it is a very useful food to keep handy for quick and healthy meals and snacks like this one.

INGREDIENTS
8 large open-cup mushrooms
3 scallions, sliced lengthwise
1 garlic clove, crushed
2 tablespoons oyster sauce
10-ounce package marinated tofu, cut into small dice
7-ounce can corn, drained
2 teaspoons sesame oil
salt and ground black pepper
scallion strips, to garnish

SERVES 4

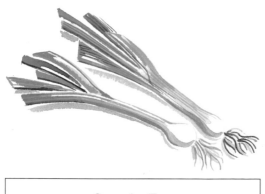

COOK'S TIP
If you prefer, omit the oyster sauce and use light soy sauce instead.

1 Preheat the oven to 400°F. Set aside the mushroom cups and finely chop the stalks. Place the stalks in a bowl, add the scallions and garlic and pour over the oyster sauce. Stir to mix.

2 Dry the marinated tofu on paper towels and add it with the corn to the mushroom mixture, season with salt and pepper, then stir to combine.

3 Place the mushroom cups, open-side up, on a plate or chopping board and divide the stuffing mixture among them.

4 Brush the edges of the mushrooms with the oil. Arrange the mushrooms in a baking dish and bake for 12–15 minutes, until the mushrooms are just tender, then serve garnished with the scallion strips

SHRIMP AND CORN SOUP

This is a very quick and easy soup, made in minutes. If you are using frozen shrimp, defrost them first before adding them to the soup.

INGREDIENTS
½ teaspoon sesame or sunflower oil
2 scallions, thinly sliced
1 garlic clove, crushed
2½ cups chicken broth
15-ounce can cream-style corn
8 ounces cooked, peeled shrimp
1 teaspoon green chili paste or chili
sauce (optional)
salt and ground black pepper
fresh cilantro leaves, to garnish

SERVES 4

1 Heat the oil in a large heavy-based saucepan and sauté the scallions and garlic over moderate heat for 1 minute, until softened, but not browned.

2 Stir the chicken broth, cream-style corn, shrimp, and chili paste or sauce, if using, into the scallion mixture.

3 Bring the soup to a boil, stirring occasionally. Season to taste, then ladle the soup into warmed individual bowls. Serve at once, sprinkled with fresh cilantro leaves to garnish.

COOK'S TIP
If cream-style corn is not available, use ordinary canned corn instead. Purée it in a blender or food processor for a few seconds, until it is creamy but still has some texture left, and use as instructed in the recipe.

MINI SPRING ROLLS

E at these light crispy packages with your fingers. If you like slightly spicier food, sprinkle them with a little cayenne pepper before serving.

INGREDIENTS
1 green chili
3 ounces cooked chicken breast
½ cup vegetable oil
1 small onion, finely chopped
1 clove garlic, crushed
1 small carrot, cut into fine matchsticks
1 scallion, finely sliced
1 small red bell pepper, seeded and cut into fine matchsticks
1 ounce bean sprouts
1 teaspoon sesame oil
4 large sheets filo pastry
1 egg white, lightly beaten
fresh chives, to garnish (optional)
3 tablespoons light soy sauce, to serve

MAKES 20

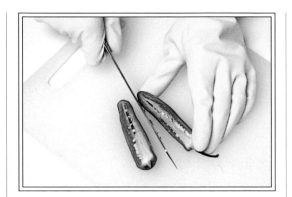

1 Carefully remove the seeds from the chili and chop finely, wearing rubber gloves to protect your hands, if necessary, as chilies can burn your skin. Avoid all contact with your eyes and mouth.

2 Using a sharp knife, slice the chicken breast into thin strips. Heat a wok, then add 2 tablespoons of the vegetable oil. When it is hot, add the onion, garlic, and chili and stir-fry for 1 minute. Add the chicken strips to the wok and fry over high heat, stirring constantly until they are browned all over.

3 Add the carrot, scallion, and red bell pepper to the wok and stir-fry for about 2 minutes. Add the bean sprouts, stir in the sesame oil, then remove the wok from the heat and leave the mixture to cool.

4 Cut each sheet of filo pastry into five short strips. Place a small amount of the filling at one end of each strip, leaving a small border at the edges, then fold in the long sides and roll up the pastry.

5 Seal and glaze the packages with the egg white, then chill them, uncovered, for 15 minutes before frying.

6 Wipe out the wok with paper towels, reheat it, and add the remaining vegetable oil. When the oil is hot, add the rolls in batches and stir-fry until they are crisp and golden brown. Drain them on paper towels. Garnish with chives and serve with light soy sauce for dipping.

STIR-FRIED SEAFOOD

A colorful and delicious dish from South-East China, combining shrimp, squid, and scallops. The squid may be replaced by another fish, or omitted altogether.

INGREDIENTS
4 ounces squid, cleaned
4–6 fresh scallops
4 ounces uncooked shrimp
½ egg white
1 tablespoon cornstarch, mixed with a little water
2–3 celery stalks
1 small red bell pepper, cored and seeded
2 small carrots
1¼ cups oil
½ teaspoon finely chopped fresh ginger root
1 scallion, cut into short sections
1 teaspoon salt
½ teaspoon light brown sugar
1 tablespoon Chinese rice wine or dry sherry
1 tablespoon light soy sauce
1 teaspoon hot bean sauce
2 tablespoons chicken broth
few drops of sesame oil

SERVES 4

1 Open up the squid and, using a sharp knife, score the inside in a criss-cross pattern. Cut the squid into ½-inch pieces. Soak the squid in a bowl of boiling water until all the pieces curl up; rinse in cold water and drain.

2 Cut each scallop into 3–4 slices. Peel the shrimp and cut each one in half lengthwise. In a bowl, mix the scallops and shrimp with the egg white and cornstarch paste until well blended.

3 Cut the celery, red bell pepper, and carrots into ½–1-inch slices.

4 Heat a wok, then add the oil. When it is medium-hot, add the seafood and stir-fry for about 30–40 seconds. Remove with a large slotted spoon and drain.

5 Pour off the excess oil, leaving about 2 tablespoons in the wok, and add the vegetables with the ginger and scallion. Stir-fry for about 1 minute.

6 Return the seafood to the wok, stir for another 30–40 seconds, then stir in the salt, sugar, wine or sherry, soy sauce, and hot bean sauce. Add the broth and stir for 1 minute. Serve sprinkled with sesame oil.

RED AND WHITE SHRIMP

T he Chinese name for this dish is Yuan Yang Prawns. Pairs of mandarin ducks are also known as *Yuan Yang*, or love birds, because they are always seen together. They symbolize affection and happiness.

INGREDIENTS

1 pound uncooked shrimp

pinch of salt

½ egg white

1 tablespoon cornstarch, mixed with a little water

6 ounces snow peas

2½ cups vegetable oil

½ teaspoon salt

1 teaspoon light brown sugar

1 tablespoon finely chopped scallions

1 teaspoon finely chopped fresh ginger root

1 tablespoon light soy sauce

1 tablespoon Chinese rice wine or dry sherry

1 teaspoon hot bean sauce

1 tablespoon tomato paste

SERVES 4–6

1 Peel and de-vein the shrimp, and mix with the salt, egg white, and cornstarch paste. Top and tail the snow peas.

2 Heat a wok, then add 2–3 tablespoons of the oil. When it is hot, add the snow peas and stir-fry for about 1 minute, then add the salt and sugar and continue stirring for 1 minute more. Remove the snow peas with a slotted spoon and place in the center of a warmed serving platter.

3 Heat the remaining oil, partially cook the shrimp for 1 minute, remove, and drain on paper towels.

4 Pour off the excess oil, leaving about 1 tablespoon in the wok, and add the scallions, ginger, and shrimp. Stir-fry for 1 minute, then add the soy sauce and wine or sherry. Blend well and place half of the shrimp at one end of the platter.

5 Add the hot bean sauce and tomato paste to the remaining shrimp. Blend well and place the "red" shrimp at the other end of the platter. Serve at once.

STEAMED FISH WITH GINGER

Any firm-fleshed fish with a delicate taste, such as salmon or turbot, can be cooked by this method. The sweet taste of ginger combined with scallions makes this dish a firm favorite.

INGREDIENTS
1 sea bass, trout, or striped mullet,
weighing about 1½ pounds, gutted
½ teaspoon salt
1 tablespoon sesame oil
2–3 scallions, cut in half lengthwise
2 tablespoons light soy sauce
2 tablespoons Chinese rice wine or
dry sherry
1 tablespoon finely shredded fresh
ginger root
2 tablespoons vegetable oil
finely shredded scallions, to garnish

SERVES 4–6

1 Using a sharp knife, score both sides of the fish as far down as the bone, making several diagonal cuts about 1 inch apart. Rub the fish all over, inside and out, with salt and sesame oil.

2 Scatter the scallions evenly over a heatproof platter and place the fish on top. Blend the soy sauce and wine or sherry with the ginger and pour over the fish.

3 Place the platter in a steamer over boiling water (or inside a wok on a rack), and steam vigorously, covered, for about 12–15 minutes until the fish is cooked *(left)*.

4 Heat the oil in a small saucepan; remove the platter from the steamer, place the shredded scallions on top of the fish, then pour the hot oil along the whole length of the fish. Serve immediately.

SHRIMP FU-YUNG

This is a very colorful dish that is simple to make. Most of the preparation can be done well in advance. It comes from the south of China.

INGREDIENTS

3 eggs, beaten, reserving 1 teaspoon of egg white
1 teaspoon salt
1 tablespoon finely chopped scallions
3–4 tablespoons vegetable oil
8 ounces uncooked shrimp, peeled
2 teaspoons cornstarch, mixed with a little water
6 ounces peas
1 tablespoon Chinese rice wine or dry sherry

SERVES 4

1 Beat the eggs with a pinch of the salt, and a little of the scallion. In a wok, scramble the eggs in a little oil over moderate heat. Remove and reserve.

2 Mix the shrimp with a little of the salt, the egg white, and cornstarch paste. Heat the oil in a wok, then add the peas and stir-fry for 30 seconds. Add the shrimp.

3 Add the scallions, and stir-fry for 1 minute more, then stir the mixture into the scrambled egg with the remaining salt and the wine or sherry. Blend well and serve immediately.

FIVE-SPICE FISH

C hinese mixtures of spicy, sweet and sour flavors are particularly successful with fish.

INGREDIENTS
4 white fish fillets, such as cod, haddock,
or flounder, about 6 ounces each
1 teaspoon five-spice powder
4 teaspoons cornstarch
1 tablespoon sesame or sunflower oil
3 scallions, finely sliced
1 teaspoon finely chopped fresh
ginger root
5 ounces button mushrooms, sliced
4 ounces baby corn, sliced
2 tablespoons soy sauce
3 tablespoons dry sherry or apple juice
1 teaspoon sugar
salt and ground black pepper
stir-fried vegetables, to serve

SERVES 4

1 Toss the fish fillets in the five-spice powder and cornstarch to coat.

2 Heat the oil in a wok or frying pan and stir-fry the scallions, ginger, mushrooms, and corn for about 1 minute. Add the fish fillets and cook for 2–3 minutes, turning the pieces of fish once.

3 In a small bowl, mix together the soy sauce, sherry or juice, and sugar, then pour over the fish. Simmer for 2 minutes, season, then serve immediately with stir-fried vegetables.

BRAISED FISH WITH MUSHROOMS

T his is a version of the French *filets de sole bonne femme* (sole with mushrooms and wine sauce), but with delightful oriental flavors.

INGREDIENTS

1 pound fillets of lemon sole or plaice

½ egg white

2 tablespoons cornstarch, mixed with a little water

2½ cups vegetable oil

1 tablespoon finely chopped scallions

½ teaspoon finely chopped fresh ginger root

4 ounces white mushrooms, thinly sliced

1 teaspoon light brown sugar

1 tablespoon light soy sauce

2 tablespoons Chinese rice wine or dry sherry

1 tablespoon brandy

½ cup chicken broth

salt

few drops of sesame oil, to serve

SERVES 4

1 Trim off the soft bones along the edge of the fish, but leave the skin on. Cut each fillet into bite-size pieces. Put a little salt, the egg white and about half of the cornstarch paste into a small bowl and mix together. Coat the fish pieces in the mixture.

2 Heat the oil in a wok until medium-hot, add the fish pieces one at a time and stir gently so they do not stick. Remove after about 1 minute and drain. Pour off all but 2 tablespoons of oil. Stir-fry the scallions, ginger, and mushrooms for 1 minute.

3 Add the sugar, light soy sauce, rice wine or sherry, the brandy, and broth and bring to a boil. Add the fish pieces and braise for 1 minute. Thicken with the remaining cornstarch paste and sprinkle with sesame oil. Serve immediately.

STIR-FRIED BEEF WITH ORANGE AND GINGER

Stir-frying uses the minimum of fat and it is also one of the quickest ways to cook, but you do need to choose very tender meat.

INGREDIENTS
*1 pound lean beef rump, fillet or sirloin,
cut into thin strips
finely shredded rind and juice of
1 orange
1 tablespoon light soy sauce
1 teaspoon cornstarch
1-inch piece fresh ginger root,
finely chopped
2 teaspoons sesame oil
1 large carrot, cut into thin strips
2 scallions, thinly sliced
rice noodles or boiled rice, to serve*

SERVES 4

1 Place the beef strips in a bowl and sprinkle over the orange rind and juice. Cover and leave to marinate for at least 30 minutes, stirring from time to time.

2 Drain the marinade from the meat and reserve the marinade. Mix the meat with the soy sauce, cornstarch, and ginger.

COOK'S TIP
To extract the maximum amount of juice from an orange, warm it for a short while in the oven, then roll it backward and forward with your hand before squeezing.

3 Heat the sesame oil in a wok or large frying pan. When it is hot, add the beef strips and stir-fry for 1 minute until they are lightly colored. Add the carrot strips and stir-fry for another 2–3 minutes.

4 Stir in the sliced scallions and the reserved marinade, then cook over medium heat, stirring constantly, until the sauce is boiling, thickened and glossy. Serve the stir-fried beef immediately, accompanied by a serving of rice noodles, or just plain boiled rice.

SWEET-AND-SOUR LAMB

This recipe from the Imperial kitchens of the Manchu Dynasty is perhaps a forerunner of today's favorite sweet-and-sour pork.

INGREDIENTS

10–12 ounces boneless leg of lamb
1 tablespoon yellow bean sauce
vegetable oil, for deep-frying
½ teaspoon finely chopped fresh ginger root
½ cucumber, thinly sliced
1 tablespoon light soy sauce
1 tablespoon Chinese rice wine or dry sherry
2 tablespoons rice vinegar
2 tablespoons light brown sugar
3–4 tablespoons chicken broth or water
1 tablespoon cornstarch, mixed with a little water
½ teaspoon sesame oil

SERVES 4

1 Cut the lamb into thin 1-inch slices. Place the lamb slices in a bowl, and mix with the yellow bean sauce. Leave to marinate for 35–40 minutes, stirring from time to time.

2 Heat the oil in a wok, and deep-fry the lamb for about 30–40 seconds or until the color changes. Remove with a slotted spoon and drain well.

3 Pour off the excess oil, leaving about ½ tablespoon. Add the ginger, cucumber, soy sauce, wine or sherry, vinegar, sugar, stock, cornstarch paste, and sesame oil and stir until smooth *(left)*. Add the lamb, blend well, and serve immediately.

GINGER PORK WITH BLACK BEAN SAUCE

T he combination of the sweetness of bell peppers and the saltiness of preserved black beans gives this dish a wonderful, distinctive flavor.

INGREDIENTS
12 ounces pork fillet
1 garlic clove, crushed
1 tablespoon shredded fresh ginger root
6 tablespoons chicken broth
2 tablespoons dry sherry
1 tablespoon light soy sauce
1 teaspoon sugar
2 teaspoons cornstarch
3 tablespoons peanut oil
2 yellow bell peppers, seeded and cut into strips
2 red bell peppers, seeded and cut into strips
1 bunch scallions, sliced diagonally
3 tablespoons preserved black beans, coarsely chopped
fresh cilantro, to garnish (optional)

SERVES 4

1 Cut the pork into thin slices across the grain of the meat. Put the slices into a bowl and mix them with the garlic and the ginger. Leave the pork to marinate at room temperature for 15 minutes.

2 Blend together the broth, sherry, soy sauce, sugar, and cornstarch in a small bowl, then set the sauce mixture aside.

3 Heat the oil in a wok or large frying pan, add the marinated pork and stir-fry for 2–3 minutes. Add the bell peppers and scallions and stir-fry for another 2 minutes *(left)*. Add the beans and sauce mixture and cook, stirring, until thick. Serve hot, garnished with fresh cilantro, if using.

Mu Shu Pork with Eggs and Mushrooms

In Chinese *Mu Shu* is the name for a bright yellow flower. Traditionally, this dish is served as a filling wrapped in thin pancakes, but it can also be served on its own with plain rice.

Ingredients

½ ounce dried wood-ear mushrooms
6–8 ounces pork tenderloin
8 ounces Napa cabbage
4-ounce can bamboo shoots, drained
2 scallions
3 eggs
1 teaspoon salt
4 tablespoons vegetable oil
1 tablespoon light soy sauce
1 tablespoon Chinese rice wine or dry sherry
few drops of sesame oil, to serve

Serves 4

1 Soak the mushrooms in a bowl of cold water for 25–30 minutes, then rinse thoroughly and discard any hard stalks. Drain the mushrooms, then thinly slice. Cut the pork into matchstick pieces. Thinly shred the Napa cabbage, bamboo shoots, and scallions.

2 Break the eggs into a bowl, add a pinch of salt, and beat. Heat a little oil in a wok, add the eggs and stir and turn gently until lightly scrambled but not at all dry. Remove, set aside, and keep warm.

3 Heat the remaining oil in the wok, add the pork and stir-fry for about 1 minute, or until the color changes. Add the mushrooms, Napa cabbage, bamboo shoots, and scallions and stir-fry for 1 minute more, then add the remaining salt, the soy sauce, and wine or sherry.

4 Stir-fry the vegetables for 1 minute more before returning the scrambled eggs to the wok. Break up the eggs and blend in well with the pork and vegetables. Sprinkle with sesame oil and serve immediately.

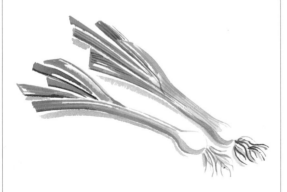

DRY-FRIED SHREDDED BEEF

D ry-frying is a unique Szechuan cooking method, in which the main ingredient is first stir-fried slowly over low heat until dry, then finished quickly with the other ingredients over high heat.

INGREDIENTS
12–14 ounces lean beef
1 large or 2 small carrots
2–3 celery stalks
2 tablespoons sesame oil
1 tablespoon Chinese rice wine or dry sherry
1 tablespoon hot bean sauce
1 tablespoon light soy sauce
1 garlic clove, finely chopped
1 teaspoon light brown sugar
2–3 scallions, finely chopped
½ teaspoon finely chopped fresh ginger root
ground Szechuan peppercorns, to taste

SERVES 4

1 Using a cleaver or a very sharp knife, slice the beef into matchstick shreds. Thinly shred the carrots and celery into pieces about the same size.

2 Heat a wok, then add the sesame oil (it will smoke very quickly). Reduce the heat and stir-fry the beef shreds with the wine or sherry until the color changes.

3 Pour off the excess liquid from the wok and reserve. Continue stirring until the meat is absolutely dry.

4 Add the hot bean sauce, soy sauce, garlic, and sugar. Blend thoroughly, then add the carrot and celery shreds.

5 Increase the heat to high and add the scallions, ginger, and the reserved cooking liquid. Continue stirring and, when all the juice has evaporated, season with Szechuan pepper and serve.

STIR-FRIED PORK WITH VEGETABLES

This is a basic recipe for cooking any meat with any vegetables in an authentic Chinese style.

INGREDIENTS
8 ounces pork tenderloin
1 tablespoon light soy sauce
1 teaspoon light brown sugar
1 teaspoon Chinese rice wine or
dry sherry
2 teaspoons cornstarch mixed with a
little water
4 ounces snow peas
4 ounces mushrooms
1 large or 2 small carrots
1 scallion
4 tablespoons vegetable oil
1 teaspoon salt
chicken broth or water, if necessary
few drops of sesame oil, to serve

SERVES 4

1 Using a sharp knife, cut the pork into thin 1-inch slices. Marinate with about 1 teaspoon of the soy sauce, the sugar, wine or sherry, and cornstarch paste.

2 Top and tail the snow peas; thinly slice the mushrooms; cut the carrots into pieces that are roughly the same size as the pork, and cut the scallion diagonally into short sections.

3 Heat a wok, then add the oil. When it is hot, add the pork and stir-fry for about 1 minute or until its color changes. Remove with a slotted spoon and keep warm.

4 Put the prepared vegetables into the wok and cook, stirring and turning, for about 2 minutes.

5 Add the salt and the partly cooked pork, and a little broth or water only if necessary. Continue stirring for another 1–2 minutes, then add the remaining soy sauce and blend thoroughly. Sprinkle with sesame oil and serve immediately.

CRISPY AROMATIC DUCK

Because this dish is often served with pancakes, scallions, cucumber, and duck sauce or plum sauce, many people mistakenly think it is Peking duck. This recipe, however, uses a quite different cooking method. The result is just as crispy but the delightful aroma makes this dish particularly distinctive. Thin pancakes are widely available from Chinese stores and delicatessens.

INGREDIENTS

1 oven-ready duckling, weighing about
4½–5 pounds
2 teaspoons salt
5–6 whole star anise
1 tablespoon Szechuan peppercorns
1 teaspoon cloves
2–3 cinnamon sticks
3–4 scallions
3–4 slices fresh ginger root, unpeeled
5–6 tablespoons Chinese rice wine or
dry sherry
vegetable oil, for deep-frying
lettuce leaves, to garnish
12–16 thin pancakes, plum sauce,
½ bunch shredded scallions,
½ cucumber cut into matchstick
strips, to serve

SERVES 6–8

1 Remove the wings from the duck. Split the body in half down the backbone. Rub salt all over the two duck halves, taking care to rub it well in. Place the duck in a dish with the spices, the scallions, ginger root, and rice wine or sherry. Leave the duck to marinate for at least 4–6 hours, or longer if you have time, turning occasionally.

2 Steam the duck vigorously with the marinade for 3–4 hours (longer if possible), then remove from the cooking liquid and leave to cool, covered, for at least 5–6 hours. The duck must be completely cold and dry or the skin will not be crispy.

3 Heat the oil in a wok until smoking, place the duck pieces in the oil, skin-side down, and deep-fry for 5–6 minutes or until crisp and brown, turning just once at the very last moment.

4 Remove the duck from the wok with a slotted spoon and drain on paper towels. Arrange the lettuce leaves on a large platter. To serve, place the duck on the lettuce and remove from the bone at the table or before serving. Each guest places a few pieces of meat on a pancake, adds some sauce, shredded scallion, and cucumber, then rolls up the pancake.

"KUNG PO" CHICKEN – SZECHUAN STYLE

Kung Po was the name of a court official in Szechuan; his cook created this dish. Omit some or all of the chilies for a less spicy dish.

INGREDIENTS

12 ounces chicken thighs, boned and skinned
¼ teaspoon salt
½ egg white, lightly beaten
2 teaspoons cornstarch, mixed with water
1 green bell pepper, cored and seeded
4 tablespoons vegetable oil
3–4 whole dried red chilies, soaked in water for 10 minutes
1 scallion, cut into short sections
few small pieces of fresh ginger root, peeled
1 tablespoon sweet bean paste or hoisin sauce
1 teaspoon hot bean paste
1 tablespoon Chinese rice wine or dry sherry
1 cup roasted cashews, and a few drops of sesame oil, to serve

SERVES 4

1 Cut the chicken into ½-inch cubes. In a bowl, mix the chicken with the salt, egg white, and cornstarch paste. Cut the green bell pepper into squares about the same size as the chicken cubes.

2 Heat a wok, then add the oil. When it is hot, add the chicken cubes and stir-fry for about 1 minute, or until the color changes. Remove the chicken from the wok with a slotted spoon and keep warm.

3 Add the green bell pepper, soaked red chilies, scallion, and ginger and stir-fry for about 1 minute.

4 Add the chicken to the wok with the sweet bean paste or hoi-sin sauce, hot bean paste, and wine or sherry. Blend - thoroughly and cook for 1 minute more. Finally stir in the cashews and sesame oil. Transfer to a warmed serving platter and serve immediately.

CHICKEN AND VEGETABLE STIR-FRY

M ake this quick supper dish a little hotter and spicier by adding either more fresh ginger root or more oyster sauce, if you wish.

INGREDIENTS
rind of ½ lemon
½-inch piece of fresh ginger root
1 large garlic clove
2 tablespoons sunflower oil
10 ounces lean chicken, thinly sliced
½ red bell pepper, seeded and sliced
½ green bell pepper, seeded and sliced
4 scallions, chopped
2 carrots, cut into matchsticks
4 ounces fine green beans
2 tablespoons oyster sauce
pinch of sugar
¼ cup salted peanuts, lightly crushed
salt and ground black pepper
fresh cilantro leaves, to garnish
rice, to serve

SERVES 4

1 Thinly slice the lemon rind. Peel and chop the ginger and garlic. Heat the oil in a frying pan or wok over high heat. Add the lemon rind, ginger, and garlic, and stir-fry for 30 seconds until brown.

2 Add the chicken and stir-fry for about 2 minutes. Add the vegetables *(left)* and stir-fry for 4–5 minutes, until the chicken is cooked and the vegetables are tender.

3 Finally stir in the oyster sauce, sugar, peanuts, and seasoning to taste and stir-fry for another minute to mix and blend well. Serve at once, sprinkled with the cilantro leaves and accompanied by rice.

CHICKEN WITH CHINESE VEGETABLES

T he chicken in this recipe can be replaced by almost any other meat, such as pork, beef, or liver – or you can even use shrimp, if you prefer.

INGREDIENTS

8–10 ounces chicken, boned and skinned
1 teaspoon salt
½ egg white, lightly beaten
2 teaspoons cornstarch, mixed with a little water
4 tablespoons vegetable oil
6–8 small dried shiitake mushrooms, soaked
4-ounce can bamboo shoots, sliced
4 ounces snow peas, trimmed
1 scallion, cut into short sections
a few small pieces fresh ginger root, peeled
1 teaspoon light brown sugar
1 tablespoon light soy sauce
1 tablespoon Chinese rice wine or dry sherry
few drops of sesame oil, to serve

SERVES 4

1 Cut the chicken into thin 1-inch slices. In a bowl, mix a pinch of the salt with the egg white and cornstarch paste.

2 Heat a wok, then add the oil. When it is hot, add the chicken slices and stir-fry over medium heat for about 30 seconds, then, using a slotted spoon, transfer to a plate and keep warm.

3 Add the mushrooms, bamboo shoots, snow peas, scallion, and ginger and stir-fry over high heat for about 1 minute. Add the salt, sugar, and chicken. Blend together, then add the soy sauce and wine or sherry. Stir a few more times, then sprinkle with the sesame oil and serve.

STIR-FRIED TURKEY WITH SNOW PEAS

The crunchiness of the snow peas, water chestnuts, scallions, and cashews gives this turkey dish an interesting texture.

INGREDIENTS

2 tablespoons sesame oil

6 tablespoons lemon juice

1 garlic clove, crushed

½-inch piece fresh ginger root, peeled and shredded

1 teaspoon clear honey

1 pound turkey fillets, cut into strips

4 ounces snow peas, trimmed

2 tablespoons peanut oil

½ cup cashews

6 scallions, cut into strips

8-ounce can water chestnuts, drained and thinly sliced

salt

saffron rice, to serve

SERVES 4

1 Mix together the sesame oil, lemon juice, garlic, ginger, and honey in a shallow non-metallic dish. Add the turkey and mix well. Cover and leave to marinate for 3–4 hours, stirring occasionally.

2 Blanch the snow peas in boiling salted water for 1 minute. Drain and refresh under cold running water.

3 Drain the marinade from the turkey strips and reserve the marinade. Heat the peanut oil in a wok or large frying pan, add the cashews and stir-fry for about 1–2 minutes, until golden brown. Using a slotted spoon, remove the cashews from the wok and set them aside.

4 Add the turkey strips to the wok and stir-fry for 3–4 minutes, until they are golden brown on all sides. Add the scallions, snow peas, and water chestnuts and pour in the reserved marinade. Cook for a few minutes, until the turkey is tender and the sauce is bubbling and hot.

5 Return the nuts to the wok and stir in. Transfer to a warmed serving platter and serve immediately, with saffron rice.

SOY-BRAISED CHICKEN

This dish can be served hot or cold. Soy sauce is a vital ingredient in Chinese cooking. Light soy sauce is thinner and saltier than the dark variety.

INGREDIENTS

1 whole chicken, weighing about 3–3½ pounds

1 tablespoon ground Szechuan peppercorns

2 tablespoons finely chopped fresh ginger root

3 tablespoons light soy sauce

2 tablespoons dark soy sauce

3 tablespoons Chinese rice wine or sherry

1 tablespoon crystallized sugar

vegetable oil, for deep-frying

2½ cups chicken broth or water

2 teaspoons salt

1 ounce sugar

lettuce leaves, to garnish

SERVES 6–8
AS PART OF A LARGER MEAL

1 Rub the chicken, both inside and out, with the Szechuan pepper and ginger. Marinate the bird with the soy sauces, wine or sherry, and sugar for 3 hours, turning the bird several times.

2 Heat a wok, then add the oil. When it is hot, add the chicken, reserving the marinade, and deep-fry for 5–6 minutes, or until brown all over.

3 Remove and drain. Pour off the excess oil, add the marinade with the broth or water, salt, and the sugar and bring to a boil. Return the chicken to the wok and braise in the sauce, covered, for 35–40 minutes, turning once or twice.

4 Remove the chicken and let cool a little before chopping it into about 30 bite-size pieces. Arrange the chicken pieces on a bed of lettuce leaves, then pour some of the sauce over and serve at once. Use the remaining sauce another time.

POK CHOI AND MUSHROOM STIR-FRY

Try to buy all the mushrooms, if you can, as the variety of flavors gives great subtlety to the finished dish; the oyster and shiitake mushrooms have particularly distinctive flavors.

INGREDIENTS
4 dried black Chinese mushrooms
1 pound pok choi
2 ounces oyster mushrooms
2 ounces shiitake mushrooms
1 tablespoon vegetable oil
1 garlic clove, crushed
2 tablespoons oyster sauce

SERVES 4

COOK'S TIP
Pok or pak choi is a type of cabbage with long thin stems and dark green leaves. Bok choi can be used instead. The leaves are crisper but the flavor is very similar.

1 Put the dried black Chinese mushrooms into a small bowl and pour over ⅔ cup boiling water. Leave for about 15 minutes to let the mushrooms soften.

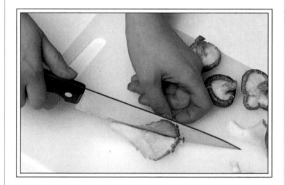

2 Meanwhile, tear the pok choi into bite-size pieces with your fingers. Using a sharp knife, halve any large oyster or shiitake mushrooms.

3 Strain the Chinese mushrooms. Heat the wok, then add the oil. When hot, stir-fry the garlic, until softened but not colored.

4 Add the pok choi and stir-fry for about 1 minute. Mix in all the mushrooms and stir-fry for 1 minute. Finally, add the oyster sauce, toss well and serve immediately.

VARIATION
Braise the mushrooms in a well-flavored sauce. Omit the pok choi. Heat 1 tablespoon oil in a wok, add a selection of mushrooms and stir-fry for 1 minute, then add 2 tablespoons each of dark soy sauce, Chinese rice wine or dry sherry and sugar, 1 teaspoon sesame oil, and 1¼ cups chicken or vegetable broth. Reduce the heat and braise, stirring, for 5–7 minutes, until the liquid has almost evaporated.

STIR-FRIED MIXED VEGETABLES

When selecting different items for a dish, never mix ingredients indiscriminately. In their cooking, as in all things, the Chinese aim to achieve a harmonious balance of color and texture.

INGREDIENTS
8 ounces Napa cabbage
4 ounces baby corn
4 ounces broccoli
1 large or 2 small carrots
4 tablespoons vegetable oil
1 teaspoon salt
1 teaspoon light brown sugar
chicken broth or water, if necessary
1 tablespoon light soy sauce
few drops of sesame oil (optional)

SERVES 4

1 Cut the Napa cabbage into thick slices. Cut the baby corn lengthwise, if wished. Separate the broccoli into florets and slice the carrots diagonally.

2 Heat the oil in a wok, add the Napa cabbage, corn, broccoli, and carrots and stir-fry for about 2 minutes.

3 Add the salt and sugar, and a little broth or water, if necessary, so the vegetables do not dry out, and continue stirring for another minute (*left*). Add the soy sauce and sesame oil, if using. Blend well into the vegetable mixture and serve immediately.

CRISPY SEAWEED

I n northern China they use a special kind of seaweed for this dish, but collard greens, shredded very finely, make a very good alternative. Serve either as an appetizer or as a side-dish.

INGREDIENTS
8 ounces collard greens
peanut or corn oil, for deep-frying
¼ teaspoon salt
2 teaspoons soft light brown sugar
2–3 tablespoons sliced toasted almonds,
to garnish

SERVES 4

1 Cut out and discard any tough stalks from the collard greens. Place about six leaves on top of each other and roll up tightly. Using a sharp knife, slice across into very thin shreds. Place on a tray and leave to dry for about 2 hours.

2 Heat about 2–3 inches of oil in a heavy saucepan or wok to 375°F. Carefully place a handful of the leaves in the oil – it will bubble and spit for about the first 10 seconds and then die down. Deep-fry the leaves for about 45 seconds, or until they are a slightly darker green – do not let the leaves burn.

3 Remove the leaves with a slotted spoon, drain on paper towels and transfer to a serving dish. Keep warm in the oven while frying the remainder.

4 When you have deep-fried all the shredded leaves, sprinkle them with the salt and sugar and toss lightly so that they are all thoroughly coated. Garnish with the toasted almonds and serve immediately.

COOK'S TIP
Make sure that your pan is deep enough to allow the oil to bubble up during cooking. The pan should be less than half full.

TOFU AND CRUNCHY VEGETABLES

ofu, also known as soybean curd or just bean curd, is best if it is marinated lightly before cooking to add extra flavor. Using smoked tofu makes this dish even tastier.

INGREDIENTS

2 × 8-ounce cartons smoked tofu, cubed
3 tablespoons soy sauce
2 tablespoons dry sherry or vermouth
1 tablespoon sesame oil
3 tablespoons peanut or sunflower oil
2 leeks, thinly sliced
2 carrots, cut into matchsticks
1 large zucchini, thinly sliced
4 ounces baby corn, halved
4 ounces button or shiitake mushrooms, sliced
1 tablespoon sesame seeds
egg noodles, to serve (optional)

SERVES 4

COOK'S TIP
The secret of successful stir-frying is to have all your ingredients ready prepared before you heat the oil in the wok. Arrange vegetables on separate dishes and measure out sauces, oils, and spices.

1 Place the tofu cubes in a large bowl and add the soy sauce, sherry or vermouth, and the sesame oil. Stir to mix thoroughly, then cover and leave to marinate in a cool place for at least 30 minutes. Lift the tofu cubes out of the marinade with a slotted spoon, reserving the marinade.

2 Heat the peanut or sunflower oil in a wok or large frying pan, add the tofu cubes and stir-fry until browned all over. Remove with a slotted spoon and set aside.

3 Stir-fry the leeks, carrots, zucchini, and baby corn, stirring and tossing for about 2 minutes. Add the mushrooms and stir-fry for 1 minute more.

4 Return the tofu cubes to the wok and pour in the reserved marinade. Heat until bubbling, then sprinkle over the sesame seeds. Serve immediately, straight from the wok, with hot noodles tossed in a little sesame oil if liked.

BRAISED VEGETABLES

T he original recipe calls for no fewer than 18 different ingredients to represent the 18 Buddhas. Later, this was reduced to eight, but today anything between four and six items is regarded as more than sufficient.

INGREDIENTS

¼ ounce dried wood-ear mushrooms
3 ounces straw mushrooms, drained
3-ounce can bamboo shoots, sliced
2 ounces snow peas
8 ounces tofu
6 ounces Napa cabbage
3–4 tablespoons vegetable oil
1 teaspoon salt
½ teaspoon light brown sugar
1 tablespoon light soy sauce
few drops of sesame oil (optional)

SERVES 4

1 Soak the wood-ear mushrooms in cold water for 20–25 minutes, then rinse and discard the hard stalks, if any. Cut the straw mushrooms in half lengthwise; if large cut in pieces, if small keep them whole. Rinse and drain the bamboo shoot slices. Top and tail the snow peas. Cut the tofu into about 12 small pieces. Cut the cabbage into pieces about the same size as the snow peas.

2 Harden the tofu pieces by placing them in a saucepan of boiling water for about 2 minutes. Remove and drain.

3 Heat the oil in a wok or frying pan. When it is hot, add the tofu pieces and lightly brown on all sides. Remove with a slotted spoon and keep warm.

4 Add the wood-ear and straw mushrooms, bamboo shoots, snow peas, and Napa cabbage to the wok or frying pan and stir-fry for about 1½ minutes, then add the tofu pieces, salt, sugar, and soy sauce. Continue stirring for 1 minute more, then cover and braise for 2–3 minutes. Sprinkle with sesame oil, if using, transfer to a warmed platter and serve immediately.

COOK'S TIP
When using dried mushrooms, first rinse them under cold running water to remove any grit, then soak in a bowl with water to cover by 2 inches.

STIR-FRIED BRUSSELS SPROUTS

A n interesting way to cook Brussels sprouts, this method works equally well with shredded green cabbage. It is a recipe which goes very well with western meals.

INGREDIENTS
1 pound Brussels sprouts, shredded
1 teaspoon sesame or sunflower oil
2 scallions, sliced
½ teaspoon five-spice powder
1 tablespoon light soy sauce
sliced scallions, to garnish

SERVES 4

1 Trim the Brussels sprouts and remove any loose or yellowing leaves, then shred them finely, either using a large sharp knife or in a food processor.

2 Heat a wok or frying pan and then add the oil. When it is hot, add the Brussels sprouts and scallions, and stir-fry for about 2 minutes, being careful not to let the vegetables brown.

3 Stir in the five-spice powder and soy sauce (*left*), then cook, stirring, for another 2–3 minutes, until just tender. Serve at once, garnished with the sliced scallion.

SEAFOOD CHOW MEIN

C how mein is a Chinese-American dish in which a combination of seafood, chicken, and vegetables are cooked separately and then combined with stir-fried noodles. This basic recipe can be adapted according to taste, using different items for the "dressing."

INGREDIENTS

3 ounces squid, cleaned
3 ounces uncooked shrimp
3–4 fresh scallops
½ egg white
1 tablespoon cornstarch, mixed with a little water
9 ounces egg noodles
5–6 tablespoons vegetable oil
2 ounces snow peas
½ teaspoon salt
½ teaspoon light brown sugar
1 tablespoon Chinese rice wine or dry sherry
2 tablespoons light soy sauce
2 scallions, finely sliced
chicken broth, if necessary
few drops of sesame oil

SERVES 4

1 Open up the squid and score the inside in a criss-cross pattern. Cut the squid into ½–1-inch pieces and soak in boiling water until all the pieces curl up. Rinse in cold water and drain.

2 Peel the shrimp and cut each in half lengthwise. Cut each scallop into 3 thin slices. Mix the scallops and shrimp with the egg white and cornstarch paste.

3 Cook the noodles in boiling water according to the manufacturer's instructions, then drain and rinse with cold water. Mix with about 1 tablespoon of the oil.

4 Heat about 2–3 tablespoons of the oil in a wok until hot. Stir-fry the snow peas and seafood for about 2 minutes, then add the salt, sugar, wine or sherry, half of the soy sauce, and the sliced scallions. Stir the mixture and add a little broth if necessary. Remove and keep warm.

5 Heat the remaining oil in the wok and stir-fry the noodles for 2–3 minutes with the remaining soy sauce. Place the noodles in a large serving dish and pour the seafood mixture over them. Sprinkle with a few drops of sesame oil. Either serve at once or, if you prefer, when cold.

EGG FRIED RICE

U se rice with a fairly firm texture. For this dish, the rice should be boiled at least 2–3 hours before it is fried, so it can cool completely. If not, it will go soggy and the grains will not separate.

INGREDIENTS
3 eggs
1 teaspoon salt
2 scallions, finely chopped
2–3 tablespoons vegetable oil
1 pound cooked rice
4 ounces peas

SERVES 4

1 In a bowl, lightly beat the eggs with a pinch of the salt and just a few pieces of the scallions.

2 Heat the oil in a saucepan or wok. When it is hot, add the egg mixture and stir and turn gently until the eggs are scrambled.

3 Add the rice and stir so that the grains are separated. Stir in remaining salt and peas. Top with the remaining scallions and serve.

NOODLES WITH VEGETABLES

T his dish makes a delicious vegetarian supper on its own, or serve it as a side-dish with a main course of fish, meat, or poultry.

INGREDIENTS

8 ounces egg noodles
1 tablespoon sesame oil
3 tablespoons peanut oil
2 garlic cloves, thinly sliced
1-inch piece fresh ginger root,
finely chopped
2 fresh red chilies, seeded and sliced
4 ounces broccoli, broken into
small florets
4 ounces baby corn
6 ounces shiitake or oyster
mushrooms, sliced
1 bunch scallions, sliced
4 ounces pok choi or Napa
cabbage, shredded
4 ounces bean sprouts
1–2 tablespoons dark soy sauce
salt and ground black pepper

SERVES 4

1 Cook the egg noodles in a pan of boiling salted water according to the manufacturer's instructions. Drain well and toss in the sesame oil. Set aside.

2 Heat the peanut oil in a wok or large frying pan and stir-fry the garlic and ginger for 1 minute. Add the chilies, broccoli, baby corn and mushrooms and stir-fry for another 2 minutes.

3 Add the sliced scallions, shredded pok choi or cabbage, and the bean sprouts to the wok. Stir-fry the vegetables for about 2 minutes.

4 Toss in the noodles, soy sauce, and black pepper. Continue to cook over high heat for 2–3 minutes, until the ingredients are well mixed and warmed through. Serve at once.

NOODLES WITH CHICKEN, SHRIMP, AND HAM

E gg noodles can be cooked up to 24 hours in advance and kept in a bowl of cold water. If you cannot find Chinese noodles, Italian pasta can be used as a substitute.

INGREDIENTS

10 ounces dried egg noodles

1 tablespoon vegetable oil

1 onion, chopped

1 garlic clove, crushed

1-inch piece fresh ginger root, peeled and chopped

2 ounces canned water chestnuts, sliced

1 tablespoon light soy sauce

2 tablespoons fish sauce or strong chicken broth

6 ounces cooked chicken breast, sliced

5 ounces cooked ham, thickly sliced, cut into short strips

8 ounces shrimp, cooked and peeled

6 ounces bean sprouts

7-ounce can baby corn, drained

2 limes, cut into wedges, to garnish

1 small bunch fresh cilantro, finely chopped, to garnish

SERVES 4–6

1 Cook the noodles according to the manufacturer's instructions. Drain and set aside until needed.

2 Heat the oil in a wok. When it is hot, add the onion, garlic, and ginger and stir-fry until soft. Add the chestnuts, soy sauce, fish sauce or chicken broth, chicken, ham, and shrimp. Stir to combine well.

3 Add the noodles, bean sprouts, and corn. Stir-fry for 6–8 minutes, then serve immediately with lime wedges for squeezing and garnished with cilantro.

SPECIAL FRIED RICE

S pecial Fried Rice is an elaborate dish that is almost a meal in itself. To serve it as a light lunch or supper dish, increase the quantities of shrimp and ham.

INGREDIENTS
2 ounces cooked, peeled shrimp
2 ounces cooked ham or prosciutto
3 eggs
1 teaspoon salt
2 scallions, finely chopped
4 tablespoons vegetable oil
4 ounces peas
1 tablespoon light soy sauce
1 tablespoon Chinese rice wine or dry sherry
1 pound cooked rice

SERVES 4

1 Pat the cooked shrimp dry with paper towels. Using a sharp knife, cut the ham or prosciutto into small dice about the same size as the peas.

2 Break the eggs into a bowl, add a pinch of the salt and a few pieces of the finely chopped scallions. Beat the mixture lightly with a fork or a wire whisk until well combined. Set aside until needed.

3 Heat a wok, then add half the oil. When hot, add the peas, shrimp, and ham and stir-fry for 1 minute *(left)*, then add the soy sauce and wine. Remove and keep warm.

4 Heat the remaining oil and lightly scramble the eggs. Add the rice and stir so that each grain is separated. Add the remaining salt, scallions, shrimp, ham, and peas. Blend well and serve hot or cold.

SWEET-AND-SOUR NOODLES

N oodles combined with chicken and a selection of vegetables in a tasty sweet-and-sour sauce create a quick and satisfying meal.

INGREDIENTS

10 ounces egg noodles
2 tablespoons vegetable oil
3 scallions, chopped
1 garlic clove, crushed
1-inch piece fresh ginger root, peeled and shredded
1 teaspoon hot paprika
1 teaspoon ground cilantro
3 boneless chicken breasts, sliced
4 ounces snow peas, topped and tailed
4 ounces baby corn
8 ounces fresh bean sprouts
1 tablespoon cornstarch
3 tablespoons soy sauce
3 tablespoons lemon juice
1 tablespoon sugar
3 tablespoons chopped fresh cilantro or scallion tops, to garnish

SERVES 4

1 Bring a large saucepan of salted water to a boil. Add the noodles and cook according to the manufacturer's instructions. Drain, cover, and keep warm.

2 Heat the oil in a wok or large frying pan. Add the scallions and cook over gentle heat. Mix in the garlic, ginger, paprika, ground cilantro, and chicken, then stir-fry for 3–4 minutes. Add the snow peas, baby corn, and bean sprouts and steam briefly. Then stir in the cooked noodles.

3 Combine the cornstarch, soy sauce, lemon juice, and sugar in a small bowl. Add to the wok and simmer briefly to thicken. Serve garnished with chopped cilantro or scallion tops.

AVOCADO AND LIME ICE CREAM

In China, as in other parts of the world, avocados are frequently eaten as desserts. Their rich texture makes them perfect for a smooth, creamy, and delicious ice cream.

INGREDIENTS

4 egg yolks
1¼ cups whipping cream
½ cup sugar
2 ripe avocados
grated rind of 2 limes
juice of 1 lime
2 egg whites
fresh mint sprigs and avocado slices,
to decorate

SERVES 4–6

COOK'S TIP
Ice creams should be quite sweet before they are frozen since they lose some of their flavor when ice cold. Do not store ice cream for too long or ice crystals will form, which will spoil the texture.

1 Beat the egg yolks in a heatproof bowl. In a saucepan, heat the cream with the sugar, stirring it well until the sugar dissolves. As the cream rises to the top of the saucepan at the point of boiling, remove the pan from the heat.

2 Gently pour the beaten egg yolks into the scalded cream, adding them in small amounts from a height above the saucepan. This stops the mixture from curdling. Allow the mixture to cool, stirring occasionally, then chill in the fridge.

3 Peel and mash the avocados until they are smooth, then beat them into the chilled custard with the lime rind and juice. Check for sweetness.

4 Pour the mixture into a shallow container and freeze until slushy. Beat it well once or twice as it freezes to stop large ice crystals forming.

5 Whisk the egg whites until softly peaking and fold into mixture. Freeze until firm. Serve, decorated with mint and avocado.

PINEAPPLE BOATS

A variety of exotic fruits can be used for this fruit salad depending on what is available. Look out for mandarin oranges, star fruit, pawpaw, Cape gooseberries, and passionfruit.

INGREDIENTS
6 tablespoons sugar
1¼ cups water
2 tablespoons preserved ginger syrup
2 pieces star anise
1-inch piece cinnamon stick
1 clove
juice of ½ lemon
2 mint sprigs
1 mango
2 bananas, sliced
8 lychees, fresh or canned
8 ounces fresh strawberries, trimmed and halved
2 pieces preserved ginger, cut into sticks
1 pineapple

SERVES 4–6

1 Put the sugar, water, ginger syrup, star anise, cinnamon, clove, lemon juice, and mint into a saucepan. Bring to a boil and simmer for 3 minutes. Strain into a large bowl and allow to cool.

2 Slice off both the top and bottom from the mango and peel away the outer skin. Stand the mango on one end and remove the flesh in two pieces either side of the large flat pit. Slice the flesh evenly and add to the cooled syrup. Add the bananas, lychees, strawberries, and ginger to the syrup. Cover and chill until ready to serve.

3 Cut the pineapple in half lengthwise. Cut out the flesh to leave two boat shapes. Cut the flesh into large chunks and place in the cooled syrup.

4 Spoon the fruit into the pineapple halves and serve. There will be enough fruit left over to refill the pineapple halves.

LIME AND LYCHEE SALAD

T his mixture of fruits in a tangy lime and lychee syrup, topped with a light sprinkling of toasted sesame seeds, makes a refreshing finish for a summer meal.

INGREDIENTS

½ cup superfine sugar
thinly pared rind and juice of 1 lime
14-ounce can lychees in syrup
1 ripe mango, pitted and sliced
1 eating apple, cored and sliced
2 bananas, chopped
1 star fruit, sliced (optional)
1 teaspoon sesame seeds, toasted

SERVES 4

1 Place the sugar in a saucepan with 1¼ cups water and the lime rind. Heat gently until the sugar dissolves, then increase the heat and boil gently for about 7–8 minutes. Remove the pan from the heat and leave the syrup to cool.

2 Drain the lychee juice into the lime syrup with the lime juice.

3 Place the lychees, mango, apple, bananas, and star fruit, if using, in a large bowl and pour over the lime and lychee syrup *(left)*. Cover and chill for 1 hour. Remove from the fridge and ladle the fruit salad into a chilled serving bowl. Sprinkle with the toasted sesame seeds and serve.

RED BEAN PASTE PANCAKES

If you can't find red bean paste, sweetened chestnut purée or mashed dates make good substitutes. Thin pancakes can be bought from Chinese stores and frozen, or you can make your own.

INGREDIENTS
½ cup sweetened red bean paste
8 thin pancakes
2–3 tablespoons vegetable oil
sugar, to serve

SERVES 4

COOK'S TIP
Cooked pancakes can be stored in the freezer. To reheat, warm in a steamer or in a microwave.

1 Spread about 1 tablespoon of the red bean paste over about three-quarters of each pancake, then roll each pancake over three or four times.

2 Heat the oil in a wok or frying pan and shallow-fry the pancake rolls until golden brown, turning once.

3 Cut each pancake roll into 3–4 pieces and sprinkle with sugar to serve.

THIN PANCAKES
To make 24–30 pancakes, sift 4 cups flour into a bowl. Slowly stir in 1¼ cups boiling water. Add 1 teaspoon vegetable oil and mix to a firm dough. Cover with a damp cloth and leave the dough to stand for 30 minutes. Lightly knead the dough on a floured surface for 5–8 minutes until smooth. Divide the dough into three. Roll each piece into a cylinder, then cut into about 8–10 pieces and roll into balls. Press flat, then roll each piece into a 6-inch circle. Heat a small dry pan and cook one pancake at a time until brown spots appear on the undersides. Stack the pancakes under a damp cloth until you have cooked all of them.

ALMOND CURD JUNKET

Also known as Almond Float, this dessert is usually thickened with agar-agar or isinglass, though gelatin can also be used. It comes from eastern China.

INGREDIENTS
¼ ounce agar-agar or isinglass or
1 ounce gelatin powder
2½ cups water
4 tablespoons sugar
1¼ cups milk
1 teaspoon almond extract
fresh or canned mixed fruit salad with syrup, to serve

SERVES 4–6

1 In a saucepan, slowly dissolve the agar-agar or isinglass in half the water over gentle heat. If using gelatin, follow the manufacturer's instructions.

2 In a separate saucepan, dissolve the sugar in the remaining water over medium heat. Add the milk and the almond extract, blending well, but do not boil.

3 Mix the milk and sugar with the agar-agar or isinglass mixture in a large serving bowl. When cool, place in the fridge for 2–3 hours to set.

4 To serve, cut the junket into small cubes and spoon into a serving dish or into individual bowls. Then pour the fruit salad, with the syrup, over the junket.

TOFFEE APPLES

A wide variety of other fruits, such as bananas and pineapples, can be cooked in this way. Sprinkle with sesame seeds for extra crunch.

INGREDIENTS
4 firm eating apples, peeled and cored
1 cup flour
½ cup cold water
1 egg, beaten
vegetable oil, for deep-frying, plus
2 tablespoons for the toffee
½ cup sugar

SERVES 4

1 Cut each apple into 8 pieces. Dust each piece with a little of the flour.

2 Sift the remaining flour into a mixing bowl, then slowly add the cold water and stir to make a smooth batter. Add the beaten egg and blend well.

3 Heat the oil in a wok. Dip the apple pieces in the batter and deep-fry in batches for about 3 minutes or until golden *(left)*. Remove and drain. Heat 2 tablespoons of the oil in the wok, add the sugar and stir constantly until the sugar has caramelized. Quickly add the apple pieces and blend well so that each piece of apple is coated with the "toffee." Dip the apple pieces into cold water to harden before serving.

INDEX